COPING WITH A DISABILITY

BY HOLLY DUHIG

Published in 2019 by KidHaven Publishing, an Imprint of Greenhaven Publishing, LLC
353 3rd Avenue, Suite 255, New York, NY 10010

Written by: Holly Duhig
Edited by: Kirsty Holmes
Designed by: Danielle Rippengill

Cataloging-in-Publication Data

Names: Duhig, Holly.
Title: Coping with a disability / Holly Duhig.
Description: New York : KidHaven Publishing, 2019. | Series: Topics to talk about | Includes glossary and index.
Identifiers: ISBN 9781534526686 (pbk.) | ISBN 9781534526679 (library bound) | ISBN 9781534526693 (6 pack)
Subjects: LCSH: Children with disabilities--Juvenile literature.
Classification: LCC HV903.D84 2019 | DDC 613.087--dc23

Image Credits: All images are courtesy of Shutterstock.com, unless otherwise specified. With thanks to Getty Images, Thinkstock Photo and iStockphoto.
Front Cover – Jaren Jai Wicklund, prapann, Alexander Lysenko, Mc Satori, Ambient Ideas, Ortis, xpixel. Images used on every spread – Red_Spruce,
MG Drachal, Alexander Lysenko, Kues, Flas100, Kanate. 1 – prapann. 1 & 2 – Jaren Jai Wicklund. 4 – Jaren Jai Wicklund, claire norman, Nikolaeva.
5 – 1000 Words, Jaren Jai Wicklund. 6 & 7 – Jaren Jai Wicklund, Nikolaeva. 8 & 9 – Jaren Jai Wicklund. 10 – redchocolate, alexandre zveiger, SORNDA,
Nikolaeva. 11, 12 & 13 – Jaren Jai Wicklund. 14 – redchocolate, Olesia Bilkei, Jaren Jai Wicklund. 15 – Monkey Business Images, Nikolaeva.
16 – Jaren Jai Wicklund. 17 – Andrey_Popov. 18, 19, 20, 22 & 23 – Jaren Jai Wicklund. 21 – Lorena Fernandez.

Printed in the United States of America

CPSIA compliance information: Batch # BS18KL: For further information contact Greenhaven Publishing LLC, New York, New York at 1-844-317-7404.

CONTENTS

WORDS THAT LOOK LIKE **THIS** CAN BE FOUND IN THE GLOSSARY ON PAGE 24.

My Family ♡

KAT

DAD

MAYA

ME

My two dogs, Tilly and Trish.

My name is Finn. I live with my dad and my two sisters, Kat and Maya. My dad's name is George.

My dad, Maya, and I live in a **bungalow** with a big garden. My oldest sister Kat has moved out and lives on her own now.

My Big Sister

Our House

I USE A WHEELCHAIR, SO HAVING A BUNGALOW MAKES IT EASIER TO GET AROUND.

5

HAVING A DISABILITY

I have a disability called cerebral palsy, or CP for short. A disability is when something in your body or brain doesn't work properly, which makes doing certain things more difficult.

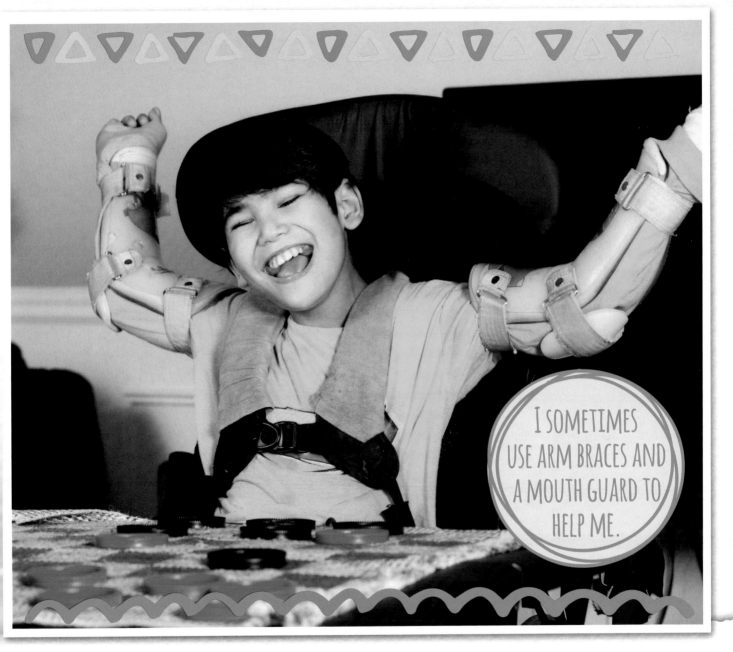

I SOMETIMES USE ARM BRACES AND A MOUTH GUARD TO HELP ME.

Having CP means my brain finds it hard to send the right messages to the **muscles** in my body. Because of this, it's hard for me to control the way my body moves.

Some things that are easy for other people can be quite hard for me. My dad helps me use my knife and fork at dinner because holding them can be difficult.

CP also makes walking difficult. This is why I use a wheelchair. I love my wheelchair. It is **motorized** so I can move it wherever I want.

AT HOME

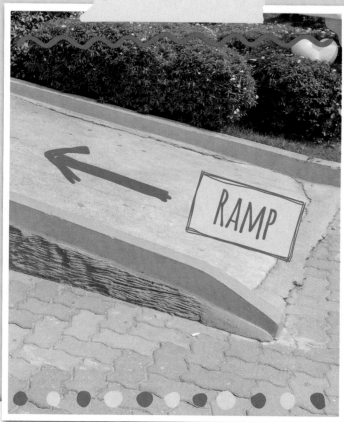

RAMP

My house has everything I need – it's great! The doors and hallways are nice and wide so that I can move my wheelchair around easily. My front door has a ramp so that I can get in and out by myself.

In my bedroom, I have lots of toys on a big play mat. My favorite toys are my cars. I got lots of cars for my birthday!

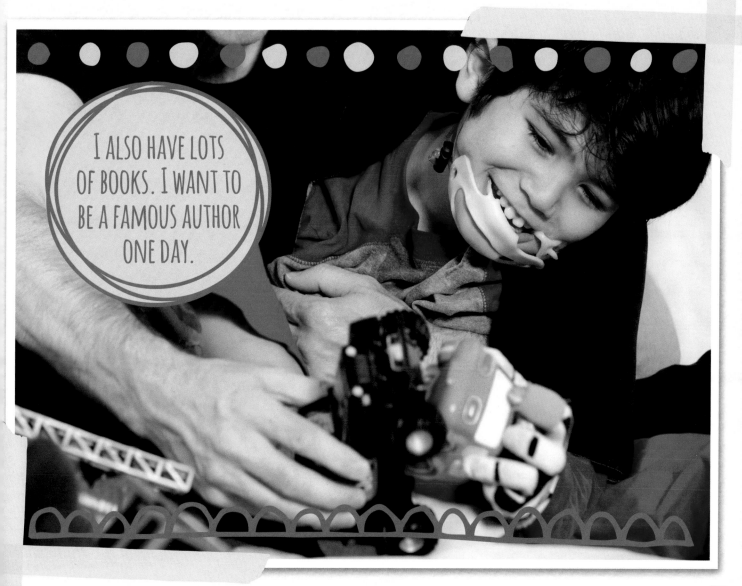

I ALSO HAVE LOTS OF BOOKS. I WANT TO BE A FAMOUS AUTHOR ONE DAY.

Out and About

On weekends, my family does all kinds of fun things. Some days we go to the beach, and other days we go to the park. I like playing on the swings.

This swing was made for children with disabilities like me.

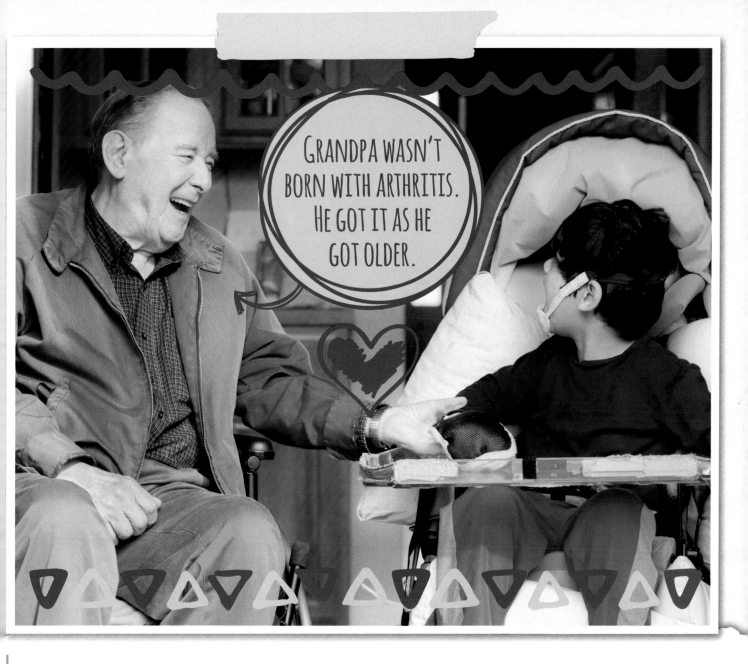

On Sundays, we go to visit my grandpa at his house and have a family dinner. Grandpa has **arthritis**, so he uses a wheelchair, too!

At School

JULIAN

On weekdays, I get taken to school in a bus that has a special wheelchair lift. My friend Julian also rides this bus. He uses a walker.

A lady named Mary-Anne helps me with my schoolwork. She is my aide. I tell her what I want to write and she copies it into my workbook.

MARY-ANNE

MY FAVORITE SUBJECT AT SCHOOL IS HISTORY.

CP means that my muscles don't always listen to my brain. This can make talking hard work, and it's sometimes difficult to make myself understood.

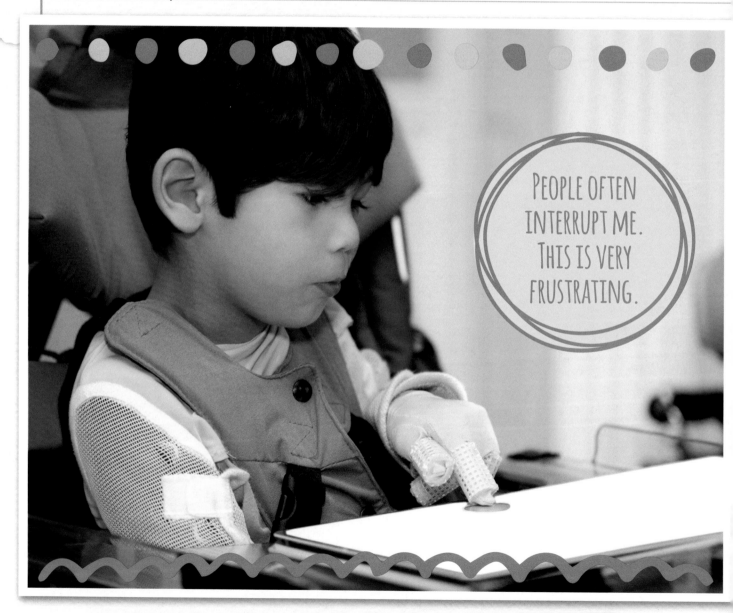

People often interrupt me. This is very frustrating.

GINA IS DEAF.
THIS MEANS SHE
CAN'T HEAR.

My best friend Gina uses **sign language**. She also finds it hard sometimes to get people to understand her. I am always **patient** with Gina.

Answering Questions ???

Having a disability is unusual, so people often ask questions about it. Normally, I don't mind answering them – I find it interesting, too!

I DON'T HAVE TO ANSWER QUESTIONS IF I DON'T WANT TO. SOME PEOPLE ARE TOO NOSY!

I don't like it when people only talk about my CP, though. There's more to me than just my disability. I like talking to my friends and family about all sorts of things!

A HELPING HAND ♥♥

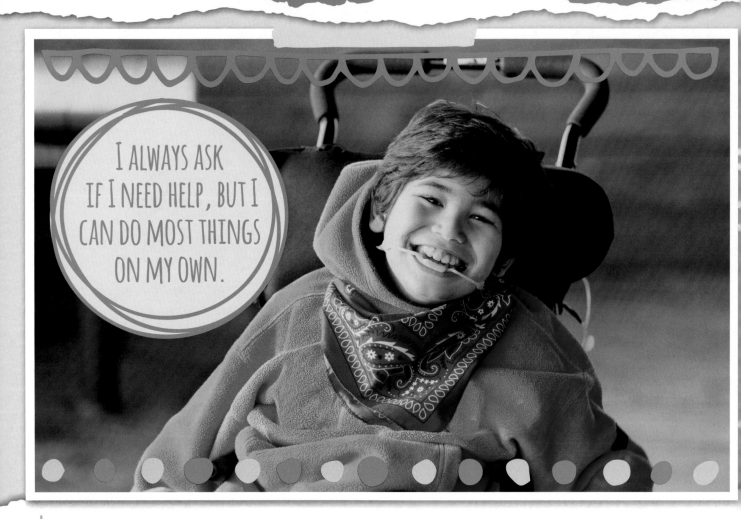

I ALWAYS ASK IF I NEED HELP, BUT I CAN DO MOST THINGS ON MY OWN.

Because I'm in a wheelchair, people sometimes treat me like I can't do things by myself. Sometimes they talk down to me, or treat me like I'm younger than I am. This feels really hurtful.

To help me become able to do even more things by myself, I go to see a **physical therapist**. She teaches me **exercises** that keep my muscles strong and healthy. I practice these at home, too.

I have CP, but that's just one part of me. I also have lots of fun with my friends and family, and I love reading history books.

Everybody has things about them that make them different. Having a disability is just one of those things. We should celebrate our differences!

Glossary and Index

Glossary

arthritis	a disease that causes pain and stiffness in the body's joints
bungalow	a type of building that has all the rooms on one floor and no stairs
exercises	activities that require physical effort
motorized	fitted with a motor or engine
muscles	bundles of tissue in the body that help you move
patient	calm and respectful
physical therapist	a person who is trained to treat problems with muscles and joints
sign language	a system of communication used by deaf people, using hand movements

Index